# Princess C and Me

## A Princess in the Land of Learn

MALCOLM R. MARTIN

## PRINCESS C AND ME
## A PRINCESS IN THE LAND OF LEARN

*iUniverse books may be ordered through booksellers or by contacting:*

*iUniverse*
*1663 Liberty Drive*
*Bloomington, IN 47403*
*www.iuniverse.com*
*1-800-Authors (1-800-288-4677)*

*ISBN: 978-1-5320-9205-3 (sc)*
*ISBN: 978-1-5320-9206-0 (e)*

*Library of Congress Control Number: 2019921135*

*Print information available on the last page.*

*iUniverse rev. date: 01/09/2020*

# *Acknowledgments*

I thank the Father, the Son, and the Holy Ghost for guidance and inspiration to reveal the truth about his creation and divine purpose. I thank the Father, the Son, and the Holy Ghost for the guidance and inspiration he has given me to think on these things as well as the visions manifested in them. I acknowledge and recognize the awesome, divine purpose and plan for all his created beings. I thank God for Princess C allowing me to express and be who I am as a giver and encourager, with the visions revealed to me. As I was led of the Holy Spirit, she received the blessings from my heart as I sought to please and obey my God. It has been a privilege and great blessing to know that God has awesome people who are real, honest, sincere, kind and down to earth. They are not afraid to believe that there are God-fearing people who seek to expose the good and divinely appointed plans He has for each of us. I also would like to thank my friend and business partner for her help and awesome wisdom and encouragement.

In Jesus's name
Malcolm R. Martin
Minister, educator and coach

# Introduction

The truth about life is that God is beauty and those he has created are the exact image of who he is and who he has purposed them to be in the world. The reason for this book is to acknowledge that real royal beauty (RRB) and real true beauty (RTB) with a pure heart can only come from God for his ordained purpose in each life. The story of a princess in the special place is important because of the need to recognize that there are ordinary people who we encounter each day that are more than meets the eye. They appear common and simple, but in reality they are royalty and do not know it.

When I saw her from a distance, it seemed as if I was watching a great story unfolding before my eyes and I was mesmerized. Each morning in the Land of Learn one could find me waiting and anticipating her grand royal entrance through those doors as she said, "Good morning." Her voice caused me to feel like a prince. When she entered and walked toward me, I was thankful for God's grace. With her words and beauty, I knew that my day was beautiful. She was the Princess of Teachers in the Land of Learn.

This story will bring to reality the thought that God's divinely appointed and created purpose for all people no matter the race, color, creed, national origin, financial status, or position in society will be revealed. There is a divine appointed and created purpose even in a common place, a place where a true princess dwells.

The inspiration for this story stems from being a teacher in the local school system and seeing how teachers and educators are sometimes not given their proper respect and honor for making life- changing differences in the lives of their pupils and others. Teachers and educators affects every area of society, from custodians, to doctors, lawyers, preachers, engineers, nurses, athletes, scientists, actors, actress, presidents, senators, congress people, and law enforcement. In this book, I hope to shine a light on the need to notice and recognize all teachers and educators for the magnificent jobs they do every day in shaping the hearts and minds of the children they teach.

This is the story about life, happiness, inspiration, elegance, style and an unspeakable beauty. A beauty that is real, inviting, strong and true. The story takes place in a special area that brings together very important people several times each day throughout the year. In this place, the little subjects come to share and take part in a necessary ritual to nourish and refuel their mind, bodies, spirits and souls preparing them for the important task facing them daily. There are workers there whose main purpose is to encourage, guide, and direct the little subjects to their specific area so that they can finish being nourished to kick start their day. This special place becomes alive when several of the subjects gather early in the morning in a place I called the eatery.

# The Eatery: The Place Where It All Began

In the eatery, early in the morning, before the break of dawn, comes the keeper of the eatery "me." I come in to begin preparation for the start of the day for those little subjects who are the first to enter the land. The early morning time is set aside for several little subjects who come earlier so their parents can get to their work place on time. During early morning, the eatery is set up with story books, coloring books, and other fun activities and games for the little subjects to read, write, draw, and color until they are dismissed to their appointed spaces to begin their day of learning and fun. These special places and appointed spaces happen in a place called the Land of Learn.

In the Land of Learn, there are specialized trained people (workers) whose main purpose is to prepare the little subjects for learning and for a future of success and service to the land in which they live and the world they will face in their future.

The inspiration of this story began when I, as the keeper of the eatery was moved from outside spaces for early arrivals into the inside place the eatery. The story begins one day as I was preparing the early arriving subjects for their daily routine of reading, writing, drawing and coloring. All of a sudden, there appeared this perfect and amazing smiling face. It was encouraging to see someone seemingly happy, and full of fun and hope. The little subject became excited anticipating a chance to embrace the one with the wonderful, smiling face, and she was amazingly and extraordinarily beautiful. In her face and eyes was an inner joy and happiness I had not seen before. What I saw in her made me not only smile but also realize that something wonderful had just happened. I saw that God had allowed me to experience true, real and pure beauty.

The events that led to the title of this story were inspiring to say the least. It was a nice cool morning in October when I saw this woman for the first time. I knew immediately that there was some precious about her. I observed every day how the little subjects, anticipated seeing her come into the Land of Learn, and they wanted to walk and talk with her and help her as she walked to her learning place. It was something I could not put my finger on right away, but I watched as they worked on their assigned activities and looked towards the entry of the eatery, quietly waiting. Then it all became very clear to me when the smiling face of the woman entered the eatery. The little ones began speaking to her and preparing to embrace her. It was amazing to see this happen each day as she smiled and greeted them. Then she smiled at me. I knew right then and there that I had been placed in the Land of Learn to meet her for such a time as this, for the purpose of bringing to the attention the awesome purpose God has ordained for each of his creations.

For the next several months, this smiling face and amazing woman entered the eatery in the same manner. I became curious, wondering who she was and where she came from, to the point that I began anticipating her entrance into the Land of Learn and the eatery each day. She not only smiled at me but also spoke sweetly to me as if she knew me. I could not wait any longer. I had to get to know who she was and what made the little subjects (and now me) want to see her, be near her, hear her talk, and walk with her every day.

I decided it was time to ask her questions: her name, where she was from, her place of birth, and her family. There was something uniquely special and precious about her that spoke inspiration into my mind and heart.

I realized that she was more than a look or a pretty face. My heart and mind became overwhelmed and full of anticipation every time I saw her. It was so powerful that I began to position myself in a place where I could see her enter the learning place each day. I refused to miss her entering the land, because I wanted to get a glimpse of her as she walked my way. It became so strong that I asked the Lord to help me understand what was happening to me. Every day I noticed her as she walked back and forth to her spaces and places to prepare for her little subjects to enter into their spaces to learn. I then noticed something that brought clarity to what I was experiencing. It was evident that she was more than a person the little learners loved. She was respected and revered by her peers. I observed how other little subjects and learners somehow knew when she was coming, and seemingly out of nowhere, they surrounded her as she walked to her spaces and places to do her responsibilities. I also noticed them as they took their places walking in front of her, on the side of her, and behind her as if they were her protectors and security, making sure she arrived safely to her destination.

This was amazing to me. They appeared simultaneously from their spaces and places to line up as if they were ushering her to her castle. It was if this was the walk of royalty. Who is she? I wondered and asked the Lord. I did not understand what I was seeing until it was revealed to my heart and mind the words royalty and beauty." She walked with a sense of elegance, style, and beauty that I had not seen before, and as a result, I was overwhelmed to the point that out of my heart and mind, and then my month, came these words: "You are royalty and beauty. You are a Princess. Thus the title of this story is Princess C and Me.

Princess C and Me is a wonderful story of the richness and power and the glory of God's creation. In other stories, people and characters whose were seemingly nobodies in the eyes of those around them, but they were actually precious people who turned out to be kings and queens, princes and princesses, and other great people. They became powerful and influential change agents in the world around them.

These are stories of great people unbeknown to the natural eye but revealed in a powerful message and experience.

The stories bring to the forefront the fact these people are jewels among us whose greatness is being suppressed and blocked until God allows something or someone to come along and expose the truth about who they are in his divine plans to expose their true purpose and destiny. The Land of Learn was filled with beauty and intelligent workers; but it is to me that God revealed the royalty and beauty in Princess C.

One morning, as I arose from my bed the spirit of the Lord revealed to me who this seemly commoner was not. She was not by nature or natural terms what one might think or imagine, but through God's eyes he described her to me. It was revealed and divinely inspired to me that she was not just a common person, she was not just a learner or teacher or educator, and she was not just given a name at birth. She was and would always be true royal beauty. A beauty not defined by an outward appearance but by an inner expression of God's grace, mercy and divine purpose for his glory and praise. Proverbs 31:30 reads "Charm is deceitful and (outer) beauty is vain but the woman who fears the lord is to be praised." God is beautiful and everything and everyone he has created are beautiful. Ecclesiastes 3:11 reads He hath made everything beautiful in his time.

I will praise thee; for I am fearfully and wonderfully made; marvelous are thy works; and that my soul knoweth right well. Psalm 139:14 KJV

# *Pink Roses*

The beauty of pink roses symbolizes the real and true beauty I see in Princess C pink roses expresses elegance and kindness, grace, joy and happiness.

# A True Royal Beauty

Every day, it appeared as if there were pink roses, carnations, and other beautiful flowers lining the path were she walked. It was as if the flowers and roses were saying "You are beautiful. You are royalty. You are a princess."

Royalty is a mindset. It is a focus and dedication to achieve and accomplish your purpose. It's a determination to start and finish the task and goals you set out to accomplish.

True royalty is being real and faithful. It is rising up early to enter into the land and make preparations for the tasks of the day and meet and greet the little subjects with an open mind, open arms, and an open heart to instruct, inspire, and encourage them to become creative and lifelong learners. It is the compassion and passion to be the best you can for all those who know you and love you.

You are a princess of learning, rising up early and staying late to prepare for the day of inspiring and encouraging your subjects and others to strive to become great.

Royalty is a mindset of knowing who you are and why you are royalty. Royalty focuses on the present, "the right now." "This is the day that the Lord has made; I will rejoice and be glad in it". (Psalm 118:24 KJV).

As the princess of the Land of Learn, you must walk in your princessness and teach others the same. Princessness is the quality or state of being willing and eager to be kind, honest and sincere as you do favors and offer others your services with cheerfulness, helpfulness, friendliness, goodness, and kindness.

# The Beginning

Somewhere out there was born a little girl who seemingly was like all other little girls laughing, playing, having fun with her family and friends, and doing things little girls do. This little girl had something deeper than her siblings and others in her life. I believe that she was the one whom her siblings and family and friends looked to as one who made things happens. Though she was not the oldest, she was always the one child I believe that her parents could depend on to get things accomplished and set in order. As she grew, she was the one who led others, helped guide them, made provisions, and for them took the blame when there were problems and consequences for not doing the right things. I believe that her family looked to her and expected her to come up with solutions to issues facing the family. This led to her desiring to learn and lead others. In high school she saw an opportunity to further her education by attending college and becoming a teacher.

Little did people know that there was a princess of teachers walking throughout their campus, and now she was in the Land of Learn?

# The Learning years

The learning years were challenging as they were for all of us. She strived to achieve goals in life. I am certain that (Princess C) was one of the best in her graduating class and was in a place to choose the best place where she would like to begin her career. She was assigned to a school for young subjects in a rural area of the town where she attended college. What made her stay there? Why did she not go back to her hometown or find another city to begin her career? I believe it was because of her God given, well designed, and divinely planned destiny. If she had decided to go elsewhere, I would not be writing this story. The story of a girl who was seemingly ordinary has become very importance to her learners, others, and me. The Land of Learn was destined to be a great place, because she would learn her true purpose and destiny.

## What Makes This Story so Important?

We live in a world where people make unfair assumptions about who they think we are. Sometimes these assumptions are based on past life experiences, which can lead to people making judgments based on family status, financial status, race, nationality, origin, neighborhood, height and weight, and other things.

This story is similar to other stories we have read about and watched on TV, which depicted people as commoners. People are judged to be important or not important in society because of social status, and/ or position. As a result, some people are considered to be so called nobodies until somebody notices them for who they really are by creation, not natural birth.

The same attitude is out there about teachers and educators. I believe this because in some instances they are not held in high esteem like athletes, entertainers, and political leaders. I believe many times they are looked down upon, misunderstood, treated as outcasts, underappreciated, and left to fend for themselves in the educational system without the support needed from some students, parents, and even administrators and educational leaders. Teachers and educators are not to be treated as peasants or second hand citizens who are less important than other professionals. Teachers are awesome people who are doing great things in their communities and making an impact on the lives of future leaders.

Teachers, like all of us, must be honored and rewarded as great people doing great things. Teachers and educators should be recognized more by businesses and companies who should offer a percentage discounts for travel, hotel stays, and all other purchases, and other events that offer discounts to military personnel, first responders, and law enforcement. Recently, I was in an auto shop to purchase a pair of new tires and asked if there were any extra discounts available. The sales person first asked if I was military or had some other status, but he never asked if I was a teacher. So I said to him, how about teachers? He paused for a few seconds as if he wanted to say I am sorry but only those I named gets an extra discount. But then, he said; I can give you an extra discount. I do not believe teachers should have to beg for extra percentages off purchases, because the work and service they render to our children, community and the world is vitally important as others. I understand that service people and first responders deserve to be recognized and honored and I salute them; but let us not forget teachers and educators who are fighting for the minds hearts, spirits and souls of our children.

Another day I was in a clothing store and I asked the worker if there was any extra discount and she asked "are you military? I responded quickly "teachertary" and she smiled and said if I was at the cash register, I would give you an extra discount for that word; no pond intended. I just responded out of my compassion and passion for teachers and the great work and service they render to our children and community and world each day. One day teachers and educators will become those we honor, respect, and pay well because of their chosen profession.

We should pay teachers and educators hundreds of thousands of dollars for performing their jobs. Why not put teachers in those places of vital importance as other professions? Without them, where would we be in our careers and lives?

# *Teachertary Defined*

Teacher and educators are like dignitaries who remain and stay in place and holds an importance position. They are Ambassadors who represents their school, community and nation at social functions, political functions and other events with the intention of smoothing relationship between parents, administration and the community.

Teachers and educators are not just servants nor are they peasants. They are powerful people who are more than meets the eye. Some teachers may not know who they are or why they were created, but they do know their role as important people in the lives of those they teach and guide each day. In the eyes of the Creator, these people are God's kings and queens, princes and princesses and must be treated with the upmost respect and honor as other professions. They show up and perform amazing tasks every day to make sure the children they teach learn and become great people. "It is great people who develop and train great people." The woman at the well (John's 4:4-26 KJV) did not know who she was until Jesus, the "Rabbi," "my teacher," came by the well just to align her with her purpose. When she learned who Jesus was and what he knew about her ancestry and herself, she dropped everything, ran into the city and said in verse 29

"Come see a man, which told me all things that ever I did, is not this the Christ? She became the first woman evangelist in Bible history.

Princess C is all about strength, beauty, royalty, elegance, and style. This was revealed from the inner person created by God for a divine purpose and divine destiny. When I think on all God has done in creation, I am amazed at the realization that God makes all things beautiful in his time and for a time as this for his glory. Princess C is a real, true, and a right now beauty. It is you, Lord, who "Make Beautiful Beautiful." The most amazing thing I have seen is the vision of all kinds Of pink roses and all types of pink flowers lined up on each side of the pathway as she walks from place to place to accomplish her daily responsibilities. It was as there were rows of beautiful well-groomed flowers and roses popping up with every step she took as she walked the path to her destination. It was an awesome sight to see from day to day. I am convinced now that the greatness of God is reflected not only in his flowers and roses but more importantly, in his created beings. I believe that what we humans think, believe, understand, perceive, read, listen to, and accept to be reality and truth is based on our own physical and natural mind set. I know that we are more than natural because of the supernatural presence of the creator.

When we look at ourselves and the perceptions we have about who we are in this world, we may realize that it is the images we have accepted, allowed, received, read about, and taught by our world or culture that have shaped our opinion of how we see ourselves and our destiny.

When God looks at us, he can only see us inwardly with his supernatural vision, and he has revealed to us and to other true beauty and purpose through his supernatural eyes. Proverbs 139 and verse 14 says, "I praise you oh Lord because I am fearfully and wonderfully made; marvelous are your works and this my soul knows well. I know this is the truth and nothing by the truth because only You Make Beautiful, Beautiful."

# *Teachers Must Be Honored*

I believe teachers and educators should be revered and honored like those in the military and other very important service jobs to our communities and country. If it was not for teachers, even the military, soldiers, and service men and service woman could not understand how to perform their duties and responsibilities. No, I am not trying to belittle the awesome jobs and the awesome sacrifices of those serving in our military, or as, first responders, because so many have lost life and limb to serve and protect us from attacks from other nations, and people who come up against us to destroy us. But let's be honest; if it were not for the dedicated teachers and educators, who are well learned and hardworking, in the trenches, on the front line of the battle against attitude in the classroom, community, and in our nation, children might miss the opportunity to become great men and women who might grow up to inspire their peers and the world. Teachers touch and serve every area of humanity.

Teachers are jewels that we must not trample over. We should build them up and encourage them to strive to be great so they may transfer this greatness to those they teach.

This story shines light on the need to notice and recognize all teachers and educators for the magnificent jobs they do each and every day in shaping the hearts and minds of the children they teach.

Do not withhold good from those whom it is due, when it is in your hands the power to act." Therefore I will take this opportunity to stand as one who will honor those who are on the front of the battle for our community, and the world.

Teachers are awesome people who refuse to let their students miss out on the opportunity to become great. Teachers are powerful change agents in a nation and a world looking for change. They spent extra hours before and after school preparing for their student's success and investing not only their time but also their finances to help assure that their students are well equipped to perform during class time and on their assessments. I pose these questions. Do you know what you know because you know it? Do you do what you do because you do it? Do you say what you say because you say it? Do you think what you think because you think it?

However you answer these questions, be sure to remember that teachers, educators, instructors and parents were there to lead you and guide your thoughts, actions, and decisions. From your home to your school or wherever you go to learn, a teacher was there to direct you.

Teachers, I salute you, Keep up the good work and do not stop teaching, because you are making a big difference, not only in the lives of your students but also their parents and other people lives.

# Teachers and Educators Must Be Paid

What is our most precious resource in America and in the world? I believe it is our children. Teachers are handling our children every day for 180 days a year and I believe that their pay is at the bottom of the scale of careers and jobs in our country and around the world. I said in the previous topic that teachers teach, touch, and influence every area of the community, society, and the world. There is no doctor, lawyer, preacher, engineer, scientist, president, congressperson, athlete, or banker who has achieved or accomplished what they have without the aid, help, encouragement, inspiration, and support of a teacher or educator. Why are these professions counted as more important or more beneficial to our world? We should value teachers above all because it was teachers, and educators who made a difference in the lives of those who lead, protect, govern, and educate our country and world.

·

# The Inspiration in This Story

We are more than what people perceive us to be, what they choose to say we are, and what we will achieve or accomplish in life. We are powerful beings created by a powerful God to show his beauty and purpose which inspires others to be all he has purposed them to be for his glory. Princess C may have never considered herself to be anything more than a common, hardworking, determined, devoted and dedicated person, but like Cinderella, she stepped out of her common place and into a palace place where royalty roamed. She found who she really was and eventually learned her purpose. This story is not told as a fairytale but a real life expression of how God can use ordinary people to accomplish extraordinary things for his glory and his praise. It is God who puts people in place, and he places them in very special places to accomplish greater purpose than they can imagine.

# Animals in the Land

It was a bright and sunny day. All the little subjects were preparing for their learning application when there was a sound of laughter and joy. Princess C had accepted the responsibility for taking on the challenge of nursing several small animals. These animals were small but beautiful creatures that needed a home and a person who would nurture them, feed them and take complete care of them. Princess C accepted the challenge and took the responsibility for the small animals. The little subjects were so excited to the point that they wanted to help Princess C with the animals, hold the animals, and transport them wherever they needed to be moved.

The day animals entered the Land of Learn, several people in the land took on a responsibility for the little animals. There were those who volunteered to construct the animal dwelling so the animals would have more room to roam, run, and flip. There were those who volunteered to take the animals' home for several days to help Princess C with their care.

# The Smaller Subjects
## Get Excited

The little subjects heard of the small animals in the Land of Learn. They wanted to see the animals every day. They wanted to touch, and hold them and watch them eat and play. They were coming from all areas of the land to get a glimpse of the animals, feel them, and even have the chance to feed them. The amazing part was that the smaller subject saw the animal as family and was willing to receive them into their daily learning. The older subjects took pleasure in explaining how the animals were named and why they gave the animals their names. The older subjects would also show the very little subjects how to hold them, feel them, and be gentle with them. Every day the very little subjects would come out in the open spaces to see if they could get a glimpse of the animals as they were transported throughout the land of learn.

Day in and day out, the very little subjects talked about the animals, what they saw the animals do, how the animals played, and what type of food the animals liked to eat. It was something to behold because I the keeper of the eatery, got to experience all of it.

# Sadness in the Land of Learn

There was a great shadow cast over the Land because a dear one to the hearts of all in the Land of Learn was gone, never to return again. The little subjects and the adults were crying and praying. The pain and sadness filled the hearts of all but there was a strength and determination to be strong throughout the Land of Learn that brought peace and even joy when the dear one was remembered. Prince C was so sad and overwhelmed to the point that she left the land to a place of solitude and serenity for several days. When she returned, she came back stronger and more determined to be all and do all she could do to encourage the little subjects and her peers to move forward and motivate each other to achieve greatness and purpose.

# Princess C's Presence in the Land of Learn

When she was in the land of Learn, the little subjects appeared to be focuses, ready to learn, and on the right track. They were eager to speak to her, embrace her, and walk with her as they passed by her each day. But I noticed several times that when she was out of the land for a period of time, they seemed to lose their focus. When she was in the land there was brightness in those places she stood and walked. The little subjects moved with a steady flow as they passed by her, and they embraced her as if she was the only teacher along their path.

It is so importance that those of us who have a special place in the lives of younger people and our peers realize that our very presence with them is precious. When we are away from them, it makes a big difference in how they respond and react every day. When we are not there, it leaves emptiness in their hearts, mind, and spirits.

# Fun Day in the Land of Learn

The little ones and all the people in the Land excitingly got ready for a day of activities, games, competition with friends, and eating great food for sale during and after the events. Princess C was actively preparing her subjects by explaining and demonstrating each game and activity they would be performing, expecting them to strive to be number one in all their events. After preparing her subjects for their events, I noticed Princess C walking down the path near me at the place of the eatery with layers of little subjects seemingly draped over her and linked arm in arm with her. It was like a walk of royalty. It was as if she was dressed with little subjects who were happy to see her and embrace her. It was as if nothing else mattered or existed but Princess C and their love for her, because they knew she loved them. They were glad that they would get the opportunity to spend more time with her during the planned fun day. This was something that occurred not only on fun day but several days a week. It was as if the weight of their hearts was engulfed by her.

# Why Was I Placed in the Land of Learn?

This is the million dollar question because I had no clue. The initial plan was to have me come in periodically and help a few times a month. Before I knew it, I was there every day, and no one had explained to me why. I thought I was simply filling in.

Two to three months into my time there, I was assigned to a building on the outer yard of the land until the inside construction and remodeling was complete. Several weeks into my entering the renovated place, the eatery, I got the answer to the question of why was I placed in the land.

In May 2015, I was given the opportunity by the Lord to retire earlier than I'd thought. I did not know why but trusted a friend who said God revealed to her that I needed to retire. I received it and decided to allow it to manifest. I let my business associate, and friend help me put in the necessary paper work. By June 2015, I was officially retired on paper. But the plans and ways of God are far from our ways, and his thoughts are far from our thoughts. Isaiah 55: 8-9 reads, "For my thoughts are not your thoughts, neither are yours ways my ways, saith the Lord. For as the havens are higher than the earth, so are my ways higher than your ways, and my thoughts than your thoughts."

The answer to this question continued until one week after being placed in the eatery to receive the early arriving subjects. It was a nice cool morning, and I talked with the early arrivals in the eatery about the procedures and the rules for the program. In walked this bright amazing, smiling face. She was to me a "right now Beauty." Her smile spoke to my heart and spirit. I felt I was there to encourage and inspire but no I was being inspired. She was the inspiration of this book.

# Princess C and Me

## *In the Land of Learn*

Telling a story of a real true beauty, a real royal beauty that is pure, honest and sincere is a great example of the nature and divine will and purpose of God to inspire us to bring light to the truth that all beauty and royalty, all people, and all things comes from God. From Genesis to Revelation, we are reminded of the true nature of a wise, omnipotent, omnipresent, and mighty God who makes all things beautiful in his time and for his divine purpose.

Why must there be a story written about the presence of true beauty and royal beauty in a special space? I believe God desires to bring to light that there are unique and different people in common places doing special things with special people. They are in the land to learn and experience amazing and life changing lessons, as well as to gain life changing knowledge that will lead them to becoming lifelong learners and life change agents for the world. There are little boys and little girls who have grown up and are in the process of being developed and trained to make a difference in the lives of others and the world. I believe Princess C and so many people do not truly know who they are, why they are doing what they are doing, or who is motivating them to do what they are doing, daily. This story is to bring to the surface the need to acknowledge and recognize those who have God given gifts and divine purpose unbeknown to them until that day God sends someone or something to encourage and expose their true purpose.

# *A Right Now Beauty*

When you walk my way, I am moved to pray.
Seeing you now causes my heart and mind to say, Why now? Why now?

Why now? Has God allowed me to meet you right now?

Why now? Has God showed me you right now?

Why now? Has God allowed me to know real true beauty right now?

Why now? Has God allowed me to see real royal beauty right now?

Your beauty is pure and shines so bright that it causes me to wipe the tears from my eyes each time you walk by.

Right Now
Right Now
Right Now

January 7-2019

# Theme Song

## *When I Saw You*

Chorus: God loves you… Yes, it's true … Every day when I pray, I'm going to say God loves you…

**Verse:** When I saw you, it was the beauty inside. When I saw you, is when I looked in your eyes… when I saw you, I got the chance to see… when I saw you Royalty…

When I saw you, I didn't know what to say. When I saw you is when you walked my way. When I saw you, I got the chance to see… when I saw you, I saw his love for Me.

Chorus: God loves you… Yes, it's true … Every day when I pray, I'm going to say God loves you… Yes, he loves you… Yes, he loves you… Yes, he loves you…

Bridge: When I saw you standing there… It was the sparkle in your eyes It was so amazing to me that I began to cry, Oh, Lord, I am so thankful to you that you let me see…True beauty and royalty. …

When I saw you over there, all I could say when you looked my way was Oh Lord; I know it is true God really loves you, and how he has created you to be what he ordained you… to be.

Vamp: God will never leave you alone. His grace and mercy will keep you strong, When things in life are looking down, you can rest assure he will be around… for you… Yes, he'll be there for you.

Verse: When I saw you, it was the beauty inside… When I saw you, is when I looked in your eyes. When I saw you, I got the chance to see… When I saw you royalty… it was so real… it was so real…

Chorus: God loves you… Yes, it's true … Every day when I pray, I'm going to say God loves you… Yes, he loves you… Yes, he loves you… Yes, he loves you…

# June 21, 2019

## *Song Title: In the Land of Learn is Good Morning, Good Morning,*

Everyday the teachers and everybody say Good Morning
**Chorus 1:** Good morning, Good morning, Good morning,
Everybody say Good morning, Good morning, Good morning,
Everyday say Good morning, Good morning, Good morning,

**Verse 1:** Good morning is what we say greeting one another in our special way
Good morning when we come to school ready to listen and to learn to have some fun...

**Chorus 1:** Good morning, Good morning, Good morning,
Everybody say Good morning, Good morning, Good morning, and "Buenos Dias"
Everyday say Good morning, Good morning, Good morning,

**Bridge**: Good morning is the special way to say, I care I am principled and ready to learn to be the best I can as I come into the Land of Learn today... Good morning to every boy and girl and everybody in our world I say Good morning.

**Vamp**: Good morning, all the teachers say... Good morning all the people in the land they say... Good morning parents and the children say Good morning each and every day... Good morning, All the teachers say, Good morning, all the peoples in the land they say Good morning, Good morning, Good morning,

**Chorus 1:** Good morning, Good morning, Good morning,
Everybody say Good morning, Good morning, Good morning, Buenos dias"
Everyday say Good morning, Good morning, Good morning,
Good morning, all the teachers say... Good morning all the people in the land they say... Good morning parents and the children say Good morning each and every day... **Good morning turn to someone**

**and say** Good morning, all the teachers say, Good morning, all the peoples in the land they say Good morning, parents and the children say Good morning each and every day… Good morning, Buenos dias" **Good morning turn to someone and say** Good morning, Good morning, Good morning, Good morning Good morning, Good morning, Good morning Buenos dias" Good morning Good morning, Good morning fadeout…

## *The Beauty of God's Creation*

The images of roses came about as I arose from my bed one morning. The vision of roses was before my eyes. I did not quite understand what I envisioned of pink roses, until the lord showed me that pink was the color for this story. I was moved to purchase a dozen roses but did not know what to do with them until the spirit of the Lord said, "Take pictures of them." I was stunned because I had never taken pictures of flowers in my life. This was new to me, but I was obedient and began taking pictures with my cell phone of the dozen roses from different angles and different back grounds going from room to room. God allowed me to capture the beautiful images of roses you see in this book.

# *The Day of Celebration in the Land*

It was that time of the year when the little subjects were recognized for their achievements and accomplishments in the Land of Learned. Princess C was happy for her subjects. She was smiling and embracing them and their families with joy and gladness. The time was at hand. The princess and her peers were preparing to leave the land until next time. They were expected to come back to the land to meet and greet new subjects. Parents and friends showered their subjects with gifts, balloons, and other items to show their appreciation for a job well done. It was truly an exciting day for all those who attended the ceremonies because the little subjects got to embrace and thank their teachers for their dedication and hard work toward helping them achieve their target levels of learning.

# The last Day of the Subjects in the Land of Learn

As I observed the subjects excitement about the end of year cleaning and the closing preparations, I noticed what I'd seen at the beginning of the year. It was when the subjects came together to walk with Princess C.

I noticed again what I call, the walk of royalty. It was evident that she was more than a person the little learners loved. She was also respected and revered highly by her peers. I observed how other little learners in the land somehow knew when she was coming and out of nowhere they'd surround her as she walked around to perform her responsibilities. I also noticed them as they seemingly took their places walking in front of her, on the side of her, and behind her; it was as if they were her protectors, making sure she arrived safely to her destination.

# Summer in the Land of Learn

The little subjects have their summer vacation and are out of the land for a season, but there are children in summer camp. There was a day that a military person came to the land, and one of the children shouted out, "Thanks for your service." It was an awesome moment and was appreciated by the military person. I asked later; "Aren't teachers doing service when they teach us?" Then I explained that everybody has to go through a teacher. Teachers serve in all facets of our community, country, and the world. Without them, the world would be in a bad place.

I say "Teachers for president!" Why? Because just like the president's job and responsibility is to serve and protect all the people, It's the teachers' responsibility to serve their students by teaching, training, protecting, and preparing them for their contributions to their community, country, and world. It is time for us as a nation to give teachers and educators their due. The word of God requires this honor. Romans 13:7 (KJV) reads, "Render therefore to all their due: tribute to whom tribute is due; custom to whom custom; fear to whom fear; honour to whom honour." Proverbs 3:27 states, withhold not good from them to whom it is due, when it is in the power of your hands to do it.

# *The Conclusion*

The presence of special peoples in the lives of little ones is so important to our society because of their divine purpose to change lives and make a difference in the future. Princess C, like all of us has a greater purpose than we can imagine. The impact she and other educators are able to make in the lives of children can make a difference in a community and in the world.

Princess C and Me gives us the opportunity to see how one person can bring joy, excitement, and happiness to children and their parents with beauty, elegance, style, and royalty. The thing that is so awesome about this story is that we may not know who we truly are until God sends someone or something into our world, and life to encourage, inspire and lift us up out our common place and then bring to light our divine purpose given to us by our Father God.

We can give praise to God because he has fearfully and wonderfully made us. It is the uniqueness and the divine difference that God has ordained for each of his created beings in order to distinguish us from one another, but he also allows us to help each other in ways that we cannot imagine.

# Glossary

appointed spaces: the special room(s) set aside for assessments

body: the physical body

commoner: the person who is living a simple existence

eatery: The room where the subject eat meals

elegance: the classy way you carry yourself that is uniquely you

little subjects: young ones

older subjects: a few years older

mind: the part of us that makes decisions

small animals: the animals that are being cared for

solitude: the inner part of you that gives you serenity

spirit: the inner part where we react to and respond to our minds and emotions

soul: the inner part of our being

spot: the rooms where subjects go to gain knowledge

style: the unique part of you those appeals to others

unspeakable beauty: beauty that cannot be explained naturally

workers: the teachers and others support personal

pure: Honest and sincere

# *About the Author*

The author, M. R. Martin, was born and raised in Augusta, Georgia, Richmond County. The author was saved at the early age of 11, and one of his biggest inspirations was his late mother, Rev. Louise M. Martin, who told him, "Remember that God is watching you," and those words resonate with him to this day. He is an ordained minister of the Gospel of Jesus Christ, and he has a deep love and passion for teachers and learning.

The author received a Bachelor's degree in Health and Physical Education from Augusta College in Augusta, Georgia. The author obtained a Master's and a Specialty degree in Education from Cambridge College, located in Cambridge, Massachusetts. The author became an educator and a coach for the Richmond County School System for 28 years and retired in 2015.

For we are God's masterpiece, created in Christ Jesus unto good works, which God hath before ordained that we should walk in them. (Ephesians 2: 10 KJV).

CPSIA information can be obtained
at www.ICGtesting.com
Printed in the USA
BVHW021816170120
569837BV00014B/935